Skills Practice

Grade 1

Mc
Graw
Hill
Education

Bothell, WA • Chicago, IL • Columbus, OH • New York, NY

MHEonline.com

Copyright © 2015 McGraw-Hill Education

Send all inquiries to:
McGraw-Hill Education
8787 Orion Place
Columbus, OH 43240

ISBN: 978-0-07-668999-6
MHID: 0-07-668999-9

Printed in the United States of America.

7 8 9 LHS 20 19

Sounds and Spellings

/er/ as in **ear**ly

Practice

earth	pearl	search	early

1.

_____

2.

_____

3.

_____

4.

_____

Directions: Write the word that correctly names each picture.

Apply

earns   search   learn   heard

5. Earl likes to _____ about the world.

6. Earl likes to _____ the map for new places.

7. Earl has _____ about far-off lands.

8. Earl _____ money so he can take a fun trip.

Directions: Write the word on the line that correctly completes each sentence.

Phonics • *Skills Practice*

Sounds and Spellings

Rule
The final schwa plus /l/ sound can be spelled *-el, -le, -il,* or *-al.*
Examples: puzzle, local, tunnel, fossil

el

le

il

al

Practice

1. pencil

2. little

3. petal

4. channel

Directions: Practice writing the *–le, –el, –il,* and *–al* spellings. Read and write the words with the schwa sound.

Apply

$$\boxed{\text{-al} \quad \text{-il} \quad \text{-le} \quad \text{-el}}$$

5. app _____

6. trav _____

7. tot _____

8. foss _____

9. met _____

10. shov _____

11. pudd _____

12. nostr _____

Directions: Use one of the spellings of the schwa sound in the box to complete each word.

Phonics • *Skills Practice*

Sounds and Spellings Review

| table snorkel think coral quilt moccasin |

1.
_____
- - - - - - - - - - - - - - -
_____

2.
_____
- - - - - - - - - - - - - - -
_____

3.
_____
- - - - - - - - - - - - - - -
_____

4.
_____
- - - - - - - - - - - - - - -
_____

5.
_____
- - - - - - - - - - - - - - -
_____

6.
_____
- - - - - - - - - - - - - - -
_____

Directions: Write the word that names each picture.

Sounds and Spellings Review

| _nk | qu_ | _le |

kett

ack

tru

Dictation

_____

- - - - - - - - - - - - - - - - -

_____

_____

- - - - - - - - - - - - - - - - -

_____

_____

- - - - - - - - - - - - - - - - -

_____

Directions: Name each picture. Write the letters from the box to complete the words.

Phonics • *Skills Practice*

Sounds and Spellings

Y_

Practice

y_   Y_ _

1. yell _____   2. yard _____

3. Do they have yams?

_____

Directions: Practice writing y_ and Y_. Write the words and the sentence in the space provided.

Apply

4.

_____

- - - - - - - - - - - - -

_____

5.

_____

- - - - - - - - - - - - -

_____

6.

_____

- - - - - - - - - - - - -

_____

Dictation

_____   _____

- - - - - - - - - - - - -   - - - - - - - - - - - - -

_____   _____

- - - - - - - - - - - - -   - - - - - - - - - - - - -

_____   _____

- - - - - - - - - - - - -   - - - - - - - - - - - - -

_____

Directions: Say the name of each picture. Write the letter _y_ on the line if the word begins with the sound /y/.

Sounds and Spellings

Practice

_____   _____

whale _____   cave _____

_____   _____

April _____   sale _____

Jake will staple the papers.

_____

_____

_____

_____

Directions: Write the words and the sentence on the lines.

Apply

| gate | game | brake |

I am part of a car.
I make the car stop.
What am I?

_____

- - - - - - - - - - - - - - - -

_____

Dictation

_____   _____

- - - - - - - - - - - -   - - - - - - - - - - - -

_____   _____

- - - - - - - - - - - -   - - - - - - - - - - - -

_____   _____

_____   _____

- -

_____

_____

- -

_____

Directions: Read the riddle. Write the word that answers the riddle.

Phonics • *Skills Practice*

Sounds and Spellings

ce
ci_

Practice

cent _____   cell _____

circle _____   pace _____

Grace has six cents.

_____

- -

_____

Directions: Write the words and sentence in the spaces provided.

Apply

face	crate	race	candle
picnic	carrot	lace	space

Directions: Write each word under the correct **Sound/Spelling Card** picture for /s/ or /k/.

Phonics • *Skills Practice*

Sounds and Spellings

$$
\begin{array}{l}
\text{ge} \\
\text{gi\_}
\end{array}
$$

Practice

_____   _____

gem _____   rage _____

_____

gel _____

1. There is ginger in the jam.

_____

_____

_____

_____

Directions: Write the words and the sentence in the spaces provided.

Apply

_____ jar   bridge

2. Kate has a _____ of jam.

_____ gave   gentle

3. Tim was _____ with the cat.

jog   stage

_____

4. We had a skit on the _____.

Dictation

_____ _____

_____ _____

_____ _____

_____ _____

_____ _____

_____ _____

Directions: Complete each sentence with the correct word from the box.
Write the word on the line.

Phonics • *Skills Practice*

Sounds and Spellings Review

| home   cones   tornado   nose   robe   potato |

1.

_____

- - - - - - - - - - - - -

_____

2.

_____

- - - - - - - - - - - - -

_____

3.

_____

- - - - - - - - - - - - -

_____

4.

_____

- - - - - - - - - - - - -

_____

5.

_____

- - - - - - - - - - - - -

_____

6.

_____

- - - - - - - - - - - - -

_____

Directions: Name each picture. Write the correct word on the line.

Skills Practice • Phonics

Sounds and Spellings Review

globe	awoke	holes	alone

7. Margo _____
late this morning.

8. Can you find Mexico _____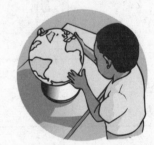

on the _____?

9. The pup nibbles _____
in the sock.

10. The kitten was _____

_____.

Directions: Look at the picture. Write the word that correctly completes each sentence.

Phonics • *Skills Practice*

Sounds and Spellings Review

bone

mule

vine

cage

note

music

Directions: Read the words. Then connect each word to its picture.

Skills Practice • Phonics

Sounds and Spellings Review

holes the Moles yard. dig in

_____

- - - - - - - - - - - - - - - - - - -

_____

- - - - - - - - - - - - - - - - - - -

Dictation

_____	_____
- - - - - - - - - -	- - - - - - - - - -
_____	_____
- - - - - - - - - -	- - - - - - - - - -
_____	_____

_____

- - - - - - - - - - - - - - - - - - -

_____

Directions: Look at the picture. Unscramble the words to make a sentence.
Write the sentence correctly on the line.

Phonics • *Skills Practice*

Sounds and Spellings Review

| me | She | be | meters | athlete |

1. Steve is an _____.

2. Leta gave the ball to _____.

3. The game will _____ at ten.

4. _____ is Pete's sister.

5. Eve can run ten _____.

Directions: Write the word that completes each sentence.

Sounds and Spellings Review

eve   Topic of a story

theme   A man's name

these   All of something

extreme   The evening before

trapeze   Not he

Steven   A circus act

she   Not those

complete   Too much

Directions: Read the words. Then connect each word to its definition.

Phonics • *Skills Practice*

Sounds and Spellings

ea

Practice

beak _____   clean _____

treat _____   weak _____

1. Can she teach me to read?

_____

_____

_____

_____

Directions: Write the words and the sentence in the spaces provided.

Apply

2. Jean reaches down to feel the cat.
   Jean reaches down on her ear.

_____

- -

_____

- -

_____

3. Peter sang a song.
   Peter eats his peas.

_____

- -

_____

- -

_____

Directions: Write the sentence that tells about each picture.

Phonics • *Skills Practice*

Sounds and Spellings

 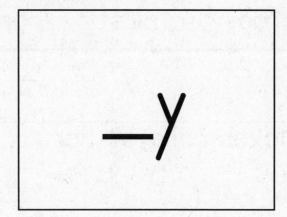

Practice

_____   _____

copy _____   lady _____

_____   _____

body _____   easy _____

I. The tiny baby is sleepy.

_____

_____

_____

_____

Directions: Write the words and the sentence in the spaces provided.

Apply

grassy thirsty pony dirty

2. Sally takes care of her _____.

3. She lets him run in a _____ yard.

4. She cleans him when he is _____.

5. Sally brings him water when he is _____.

Directions: Write the word that completes each sentence.

Phonics • *Skills Practice*

Sounds and Spellings Review

1.

y c h e m i n

_____

- - - - - - - - - - -

_____

2.

s n p i e o

_____

- - - - - - - - - - -

_____

3.

u k e y t r

_____

- - - - - - - - - - -

_____

4.

t c y i

_____

- - - - - - - - - - -

_____

5.

y n u b n

_____

- - - - - - - - - - -

_____

6.

e r s b i e r

_____

- - - - - - - - - - -

_____

Directions: Unscramble the letters and write the word that names the picture.

Sounds and Spellings Review

> thirty   babies   valley

7.

_____

- - - - - - - - - -

_____

8.

_____

- - - - - - - - - -

_____

9.

_____

- - - - - - - - - -

_____

> money   windy   ladies

10.

_____

- - - - - - - - - -

_____

11.

_____

- - - - - - - - - -

_____

12.

_____

- - - - - - - - - -

_____

Directions: Write the word that goes with each picture.

Phonics • *Skills Practice*

Sounds and Spellings Review

| sandy seashell |

1. Pete runs on the _____ beach.

2. He sees a _____.

| hockey shriek |

3. Charlie is on a _____ team.

4. The fans _____ when Charlie scores!

Directions: Write the correct word to complete each sentence.

Sounds and Spellings Review

5. The bird is near the chimney.

The bird is in a leafy tree.

Dictation

Directions: Write the sentence that tells about the picture.

Phonics • *Skills Practice*

Sounds and Spellings

cy

Practice

_____   _____

icy   fancy _____

1. Tracy eats spicy things.

_____

_____

2. Percy likes to read.

_____

_____

Directions: Write the words and the sentences in the spaces provided.

Apply

3. _____ hears the music.

saw
Marcy

4. _____ rides his bike.

Yancy
fancy

5. Nancy sees a _____ shirt.

red
lacy

Directions: Look at the pictures. Complete each sentence with the correct word from the box.

Phonics • *Skills Practice*

Sounds and Spellings Review

dance

seal

pencil

dress

celery

stars

Directions: Read the words. Then draw a line to connect each word to its picture.

Skills Practice • Phonics

Sounds and Spellings Review

| cereal | sleepy | circle |

1.

2.

3.

_____
- - - - - - - - - - - -
_____

Dictation

_____   _____
- - - - - - - - - - - -   - - - - - - - - - - - -
_____   _____
- - - - - - - - - - - -   - - - - - - - - - - - -
_____   _____
- - - - - - - - - - - -   - - - - - - - - - - - -
_____   _____

Directions: Write the word that names each picture.

Sounds and Spellings Review

| quail |
| day |
| snail |
| trail |
| way |

_____

1. It is a sunny _____.

2. The _____ go for a walk.

3. They walk on a _____ to the lake.

4. Mother leads the _____.

5. A baby stops to look at a _____.

Directions: Look at the picture. Complete each sentence with the correct word from the box.

Sounds and Spellings Review

train   tray   nails   paint   chain   spray

_____

_____

_____

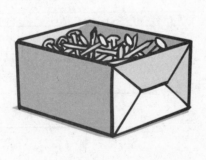

_____

_____

_____

Directions: Write the word that names each picture.

Phonics • *Skills Practice*

Sounds and Spellings

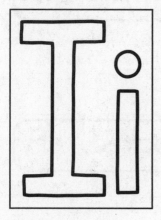

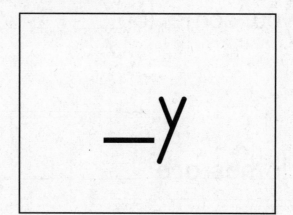

Practice

my _____

_____

try _____

sly _____

_____

cry _____

gate   apply   bend   spy

_____

1. _____

_____

2. _____

Directions: Write the words in the spaces provided. Then, say each word in the box. Write the words with the /i/ sound.

Apply

3. Can you come to _____ party?   [my   mine]

4. The clothes are _____ .   [baked   dry]

5. Do you see the plane in the _____ ?   [skip   sky]

6. The baby might _____ .   [cry   shop]

7. _____ don't you go to sleep?   [Why   If]

8. Emma is not _____ at home.   [short   shy]

Directions: Write the correct word from the box to complete each sentence.

Sounds and Spellings

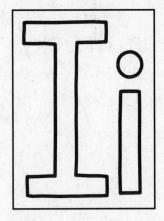 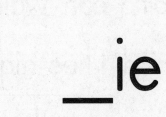

Practice

lie _____

fried _____

pie _____

cried _____

I. Mike tries to swim.

_____

Directions: Write the words and the sentence in the spaces provided.

Apply

2. The bird can walk high in the sky.
The bird flies high in the sky.

_____

- - - - - - - - - - - - - - - - - -

_____

- - - - - - - - - - - - - - - - - -

_____

Dictation

_____   _____

- - - - - - - - -   - - - - - - - - -

_____   _____

- - - - - - - - -   - - - - - - - - -

_____   _____

- - - - - - - - -   - - - - - - - - -

_____   _____

Directions: Write the sentence that describes the picture.

Phonics • *Skills Practice*

Sounds and Spellings Review

e t i

_____

- - - - - - - - - - -

_____

r f y

_____

- - - - - - - - - - -

_____

i h t g l

_____

- - - - - - - - - - -

_____

t g i f h r n e

_____

- - - - - - - - - - -

_____

r e d s i

_____

- - - - - - - - - - -

_____

p s y

_____

- - - - - - - - - - -

_____

Directions: Unscramble the letters and write the word that names each picture.

Sounds and Spellings Review

| fly | sky | lie | bright | night |

1. I am dark.

   You sleep at this time.
   _____

   I am _____.

2. I make others not believe you.

   I am not the truth.
   _____

   I am a _____.

3. I am an insect.

   I have wings.
   _____

   I am a _____.

Directions: Listen as I read the riddles. Write the correct word from the box.
You will not use all the words.

Sounds and Spellings Review

firefighter	light	tiger	fry

1.

_____
- - - - - - - - - - - - - -
_____

2.

_____
- - - - - - - - - - - - - -
_____

3.

_____
- - - - - - - - - - - - - -
_____

4.

_____
- - - - - - - - - - - - - -
_____

Directions: Read the words in the box. Write the word that describes each picture.

Sounds and Spellings Review

| i | i_e | igh | _y | _ie |

5.

sl ___ d ___

6.

f ___ r ___ fl ___ s

7.

l ___ on

8.

l ___ t

Dictation

_____   _____

_____   _____

_____   _____

_____   _____

_____   _____

Directions: Write the spelling of /ī/ that correctly completes each word. You will not use all the spellings.

Phonics • *Skills Practice*

Sounds and Spellings

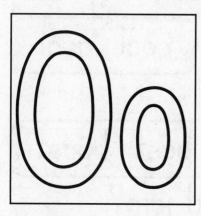

oa_

Practice Write the words and the sentence in the spaces provided.

oats _____   load _____

foam _____   moan _____

I. A goat sits under an oak tree.

_____

_____

_____

Apply Write the word that correctly completes each sentence.

2. I scored a _____ .

| coal goal |

3. Do you like _____ and jam?

| toast boast |

4. Will's boat _____ on the pond.

| groans floats |

Dictation

_____   _____

_____   _____

_____   _____

_____   _____

Sounds and Spellings

 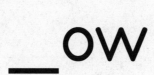

Practice Write the words and the sentence in the spaces provided.

row _____ mow _____

blow _____ snow _____

I. My coat has a yellow bow.

_____

_____

Apply Write the word that names each picture.

| snow row crow | flow throat blow |

2.

_____

- - - - - - - - - - - - - -

_____

3.

_____

- - - - - - - - - - - - - -

_____

| bow elbow tow | mow throw bow |

4.

_____

- - - - - - - - - - - - - -

_____

5.

_____

- - - - - - - - - - - - - -

_____

Phonics • *Skills Practice*

Sounds and Spellings

_ew

Practice Write the words and the sentences in the spaces provided.

few _____   pew _____

I. What time is her curfew?

_____

_____

2. A volcano spews ashes.

_____

_____

Apply Write the word that correctly completes each sentence.

> ewe   mews   few

_____

3. I have a _____ pennies.

_____

4. The kitten _____ softly.

_____

5. The _____ grazes on grass.

Dictation

_____   _____

_____   _____

_____   _____

Phonics • *Skills Practice*

Sounds and Spellings

| Uu | _ue |

Practice Write the words and the sentence in the spaces provided.

cue _____   argue _____

hue _____   value _____

I. She rescued the cute cat.

_____

_____

_____

Apply Write the word that best completes each sentence.

> value   cue   argue   hue   barbecue

2. What is the _____ of the gift card?

3. The actor waits for her _____ to speak.

4. His jacket is a deep green _____.

5. Please do not _____ with the teacher.

6. Can you come to the _____?

Sounds and Spellings Review

Practice Write each word from the box next to its definition.

| rescue narrow oak crow coat few |

1. A jacket _____

2. Save _____

3. A kind of tree _____

4. A black bird _____

5. Not many _____

6. Not wide _____

Sounds and Spellings Review
Apply Unscramble the letters and write the word that names each picture.

7.

e w m

_____

_____

8.

e r e c s u

_____

_____

9.

i l p o l w

_____

_____

10.

t f a o l

_____

_____

Dictation

_____

_____

_____

_____

_____

_____

Phonics • *Skills Practice*

Sounds and Spellings

 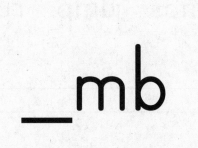

Practice Practice writing _mb in the space provided. Then, name each picture. Write *mb* if you hear the /m/ sound at the end of the word.

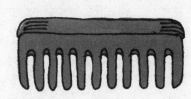　　　　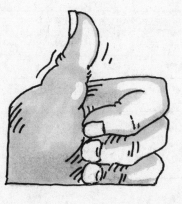

_____　_____　_____

_ _ _ _ _ _ _ _ _ _　_ _ _ _ _ _ _ _ _ _　_ _ _ _ _ _ _ _ _ _

Skills Practice • Phonics

Apply Look at the picture. Unscramble the words and write the sentence correctly.

lambs jump. run The and

_____

- - - - - - - - - - - - - - - - - - - -

_____

_____

- - - - - - - - - - - - - - - - - - - -

_____

Dictation

_____   _____

- - - - - - - - - - - -   - - - - - - - - - - - -

_____   _____

_____   _____

- - - - - - - - - - - -   - - - - - - - - - - - -

_____   _____

- - - - - - - - - - - -   - - - - - - - - - - - -

_____   _____

Sounds and Spellings

kn_
gn

Practice Write the words and the sentence in the spaces provided.

knife _____   gnat _____

kneel _____   sign _____

1. Lily can design a scarf to knit.

_____

_____

_____

_____

Apply Write the word that best completes each sentence.

> gnats   knob   knee   knot   sign

2. Tie a _____ in the rope.

3. _____ swarmed at the picnic.

4. Nate fell and scraped his _____.

5. Twist the _____ to turn on the stove.

6. A stop _____ is red and white.

Sounds and Spellings

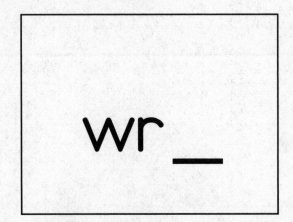

Practice **Write the words and the sentence in the spaces provided.**

wrist _____   wrap _____

_____

wrote _____

1. He wrapped the wrong box.

_____

_____

_____

_____

Apply Write the word that describes each picture.

| write | wrench | wrist |

2.

_____

- - - - - - - - - - - - -

_____

3.

_____

- - - - - - - - - - - - -

_____

4.

_____

- - - - - - - - - - - - -

_____

Dictation

_____   _____

- - - - - - - - - -   - - - - - - - - - -

_____   _____

_____   _____

- - - - - - - - - -   - - - - - - - - - -

_____   _____

_____   _____

- - - - - - - - - -   - - - - - - - - - -

_____   _____

Phonics • *Skills Practice*

Sounds and Spellings

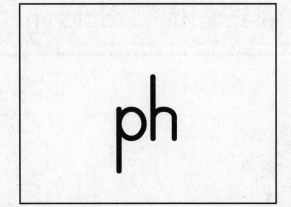

Practice **Write the words and the sentence in the spaces provided.**

photo _____   trophy _____

phone _____

1. Phil's nephew plays the saxophone.

_____

_____

_____

_____

Apply Write the word that names each picture.

trophy	elephant	dolphin	gopher

2.

_____

- - - - - - - - - - - - -

_____

3.

_____

- - - - - - - - - - - - -

_____

4.

_____

- - - - - - - - - - - - -

_____

5.

_____

- - - - - - - - - - - - -

_____

Phonics • *Skills Practice*

Sounds and Spellings Review

Practice Write the word that names each picture.

| sign write phone knight limb knee |

1.

_____

- - - - - - - - -

_____

2.

_____

- - - - - - - - -

_____

3.

_____

- - - - - - - - -

_____

4.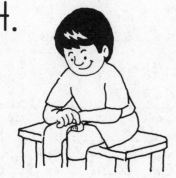

_____

- - - - - - - - -

_____

5.

_____

- - - - - - - - -

_____

6.

_____

- - - - - - - - -

_____

Sounds and Spellings Review

Apply Write each word next to its definition.

> kneel   wreck   lamb   graph

7. A baby sheep _____

8. A kind of chart _____

9. To crash _____

10. To rest on your knees _____

Dictation

_____   _____

_____   _____

_____   _____

_____

Sounds and Spellings

OO

Practice Write the words and the sentence in the spaces provided.

noon _____   too _____

boo _____   zoom _____

1. There is a moose in the cartoon.

_____

_____

Apply Read each sentence. Write the word from the box that completes the sentence.

moonlight	troop	cool

_____

2. The _____ went camping.

3. They swam in a _____ lake.

4. They sat by a campfire in

_____

the _____.

Phonics • *Skills Practice*

Sounds and Spellings Review
Practice Write the word that names each picture.

| scooter | noodles | tooth | boot | roof |

1.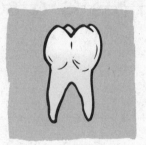

_____

- - - - - - - - - - - - - - -

2.

_____

- - - - - - - - - - - - - - -

3.

_____

- - - - - - - - - - - - - - -

4.

_____

- - - - - - - - - - - - - - -

5.

_____

- - - - - - - - - - - - - - -

Sounds and Spellings Review

Apply Write the correct word for each clue.

| moon hoot kangaroo |

6. This is in the sky.

_____

- - - - - - - - - - - -

_____

7. This is a sound.

_____

- - - - - - - - - - - -

_____

8. This is an animal.

_____

- - - - - - - - - - - -

_____

Dictation

_____

- - - - - - - - - - - -

_____

_____

- - - - - - - - - - - -

_____

_____

- - - - - - - - - - - -

_____

_____

- - - - - - - - - - - -

_____

Sounds and Spellings

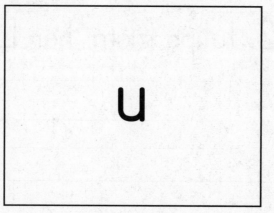

Practice Write the words and sentence in the spaces provided.

flu _____   super_____

ruby _____   duty _____

I. Susan likes to eat tuna.

_____

_____

_____

Apply Look at each picture. Unscramble the words, and write a complete sentence on the lines.

2. tulips mom. her Lucy for picks

_____

- - - - - - - - - - - - - - - - - - - -

_____

_____

- - - - - - - - - - - - - - - - - - - -

_____

3. fresh Ruby strudel. apple made

_____

- - - - - - - - - - - - - - - - - - - -

_____

_____

- - - - - - - - - - - - - - - - - - - -

_____

Sounds and Spellings

_ue

Practice Write the words and the sentence in the spaces provided.

due _____   true _____

blue _____   clue _____

1. Sue has a blue bike.

_____

- -

_____

Apply Write the word that correctly completes each sentence.

avenue	glue	due

2. This _____ is very sticky.

3. Cars drive on the _____.

4. The fee is _____ next week.

Dictation

_____ _____

_____ _____

_____ _____

_____ _____

Sounds and Spellings Review

Practice Write the word that names each picture.

bluebird	tulip	glue	student

1.

_____

- - - - - - - - - - - - -

_____

2.

_____

- - - - - - - - - - - - -

_____

3.

_____

- - - - - - - - - - - - -

_____

4.

_____

- - - - - - - - - - - - -

_____

Sounds and Spellings Review

Apply Write the word that completes each sentence.

Tuesday	bus

5. On _____ we had a field trip.

glue	due

6. When is the baby _____?

truth	clue

7. Always tell the _____.

duty	flu

8. Jack is sick with the _____.

Sounds and Spellings

_ew

Practice Write the words and sentence in the spaces provided.

new _____   chew _____

dew _____   flew _____

I. The wind blew Drew's hat.

_____

_____

_____

Apply Write each word next to its definition.

grew	crew	jewel	threw

_____

2. got bigger _____

3. a gem _____

4. a team of workers _____

5. tossed _____

Dictation

_____ _____

_____ _____

_____ _____

_____ _____

Sounds and Spellings

$$u\_e$$

Practice Write the words and the sentence in the spaces provided.

rude _____   salute _____

tune _____   fluke _____

1. Bruce prunes the spruce tree.

_____

_____

Apply Unscramble the letters and write the word correctly on the line.

2.  e t b u

_____

- - - - - - - - - - - - -

_____

3.  n t e u

_____

- - - - - - - - - - - - -

_____

4.  f u t l e

_____

- - - - - - - - - - - - -

_____

5.  u d e r

_____

- - - - - - - - - - - - -

_____

Phonics • *Skills Practice*

Sounds and Spellings

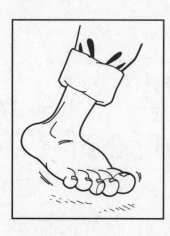

OO

Practice Write the words and the sentence in the spaces provided.

hood _____   soot _____

look _____   wooden _____

1. Come read a book by the brook.

_____

_____

_____

Apply Choose one word from List 1 and one word from List 2 to form the compound word that matches each clue. Write the word on the line.

List 1
foot wood book

List 2
pile step shelf

_____

2. A place for a book: _____

3. You hear this when someone walks: _____

4. A stack of logs: _____

Dictation

_____

_____

_____

_____

_____

_____

_____

Sounds and Spellings Review

Practice Draw a line to match the picture to the word. Write the word on the line.

crooked

_____
- - - - - - - - - - - - - - - - - -
_____

cook

_____
- - - - - - - - - - - - - - - - - -
_____

hood

_____
- - - - - - - - - - - - - - - - - -
_____

hoof

_____
- - - - - - - - - - - - - - - - - -
_____

Sounds and Spellings Review

Apply Write the word that correctly completes each sentence.

| brook | good | stood | shook |

1. Mr. Hood _____ at the ranger post.

2. A breeze _____ the trees in the woods.

3. Water trickled in the _____.

4. Mr. Hood had a _____ day.

Phonics • *Skills Practice*

Sounds and Spellings Review

Practice Write the word that names each picture.

| flute   football   tools   hook |

1.

_____
_ _ _ _ _ _ _ _ _ _
_____

2.

_____
_ _ _ _ _ _ _ _ _ _
_____

3.

_____
_ _ _ _ _ _ _ _ _ _
_____

4.

_____
_ _ _ _ _ _ _ _ _ _
_____

Sounds and Spellings Review

Apply Write the correct word on the line for each riddle. You will not use all the words.

foot   hoot   book   bedroom

I am part of the leg.

I have toes.

You can have a slipper on me.

What am I?

_____

- - - - - - - - - - - - -

_____

I have words.

I tell a story.

You can find me at a library.

What am I?

_____

- - - - - - - - - - - - -

_____

Dictation

_____

- - - - - - - - - - - - -

_____

_____

- - - - - - - - - - - - -

_____

_____

- - - - - - - - - - - - -

_____

_____

- - - - - - - - - - - - -

_____

Sounds and Spellings

Practice **Write the words and the sentence in the spaces provided. Write a rhyming word to finish the second sentence.**

_____   _____

_ _ _ _ _ _ _ _ _ _ _ _   _ _ _ _ _ _ _ _ _ _ _ _

how _____   now _____

1. Take a towel to the shower.

_____

_ _

_____

_ _

_____

2. A cow that was brown went to the

_____

_ _ _ _ _ _ _ _ _ _ _ _ _

_____.

Apply Write the word that names each picture.

cat cow crow	shower tower flower

3.

_____

- - - - - - - - - - - - - -

_____

4.

_____

- - - - - - - - - - - - - -

_____

towel howl bowl	vow town clown

5.

_____

- - - - - - - - - - - - - -

_____

6.

_____

- - - - - - - - - - - - - -

_____

Phonics • *Skills Practice*

Sounds and Spellings

ou_

Practice Write the words and the sentences in the spaces provided.

out _____   found _____

sound _____

1. A mouse ran out.

_____

_____

_____

2. The cloud is round.

_____

_____

_____

Apply Write the word that correctly completes each sentence.

| count   found   proud |

3. Jack _____ the ball he had lost.

4. Megan is _____ of her good grades.

5. Did you _____ the number of votes?

Dictation

_____   _____

_____   _____

_____   _____

_____   _____

_____   _____

_____   _____

Sounds and Spellings

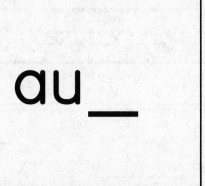

Practice Write the words and the sentence in the spaces provided.

haul _____

launch _____

auto _____

fault _____

1. The rocket will launch soon.

_____

_____

_____

_____

Apply Write the word that correctly completes each sentence.

| saucer | cause | faucet | sauce | August |

2. The _____ is dripping.

3. Paul made _____ for the pasta.

4. We go to the beach in _____.

5. Germs can _____ you to get sick.

6. The cup has a matching _____.

Sounds and Spellings

Practice **Write the words and the sentence in the spaces provided.**

raw _____   fawn _____

bawl _____   draw _____

I. The baby crawls on the lawn.

_____

_____

_____

Apply Write the word that completes each sentence.

2. He drinks from a _____.

3. The _____ has sharp claws.

4. I _____ when I am tired.

5. The dog has large _____.

Dictation

_____   _____

_____   _____

_____   _____

_____   _____

Phonics • *Skills Practice*

Sounds and Spellings Review

Practice Write the word that names each picture.

> hawk owls bounce launch clown straws

1.

_____

2.

_____

3.

_____

4.

_____

5.

_____

6.

_____

Sounds and Spellings Review

Apply Write the word that best completes each sentence.

> flowers   gnaws   hound   pauses

7. Murphy is a nice _____.

8. He also likes to smell _____.

9. Then he _____ on his bone.

10. Murphy _____ to take a nap.

Sounds and Spellings

/aw/ as in caught

Practice Write the words and the sentence in the spaces provided.

taught _____   caught _____

slaughter _____

1. Shawn's daughter is naughty.

_____

_____

_____

Apply Write the word that best completes each sentence.

vault   caught   taught

_____

2. Laura _____ the ball.

_____

3. Paul keeps money in the _____ .

_____

4. Mrs. Smith _____ math at our school.

Dictation

_____   _____

_____   _____

_____   _____

_____   _____

_____   _____

Sounds and Spellings

Practice Write the words and the sentence in the spaces provided.

ought _____   brought _____

sought _____   thought _____

I. Ollie and Jake fought all night.

_____

_____

_____

Apply Write the word that best completes each sentence.

| bought   ought   brought   thought   sought |

2. Dawn and I think Sparky _____ to have a doghouse.

3. We _____ we should make it!

4. We _____ wood at the shop.

5. We _____ Mr. Brown's help.

6. He _____ over his tools.

Sounds and Spellings

 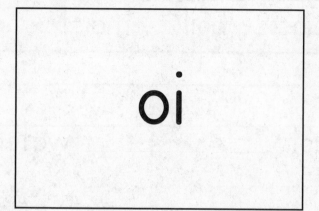

Practice Write the words and the sentence in the spaces provided.

coin _____   soil _____

foil _____   join _____

1. Loud voices made the room noisy.

_____

_____

_____

Apply Write the word that best completes each sentence.

> coins   boil   moist   point

2. We must _____ water to cook the noodles.

3. The pencil has a _____.

4. Joy collects _____.

5. The muffin was soft and _____.

Dictation

_____   _____

_____   _____

_____   _____

_____   _____

_____

Sounds and Spellings

_oy

Practice Write the words and the sentence in the spaces provided.

boy _____   joy _____

toy _____   royal _____

1. Roy has a new toy train.

_____

_____

_____

Apply Unscramble the words, and write each sentence correctly.

2. boy reading. The enjoys

_____

- - - - - - - - - - - - -

_____

3. is Joy annoyed.

_____

- - - - - - - - - - - - -

_____

4. dog Abby's loyal. is

_____

- - - - - - - - - - - - -

_____

5. oysters. looked We for

_____

- - - - - - - - - - - - -

_____

Phonics • *Skills Practice*

Sounds and Spellings Review

Practice Write the word that describes each picture.

| caught | toys | coil | thought | cowboys | coins |

1. _____

2. _____

3. _____

4. _____

5. _____

6. _____

Sounds and Spellings Review

Apply Write the word that best completes each sentence.

> taught   royal   spoiled   fought

7. Dad _____ me how to cook.

8. Throw away the _____ milk.

9. The queen held a _____ ball.

10. The puppies _____ over the bone.

Dictation

_____   _____

_____   _____

_____   _____

_____   _____

_____   _____

Word Building

> A **prefix** is a group of letters added to the beginning of a base word. A prefix changes the meaning of the word. *Un-* and *dis-* are prefixes. They mean "not."

Practice Read each word. Circle the base word. Draw a line under the prefix.

1. unwell

2. distrust

3. disloyal

4. unhappy

5. unwrap

6. unlock

7. unsafe

8. displease

9. disagree

10. unfold

11. dislike

12. unkind

Apply Read each sentence. Write the correct prefix to complete the word.

> un-   dis-

13. Emily _____ zipped her coat.

14. Max _____ likes carrots.

15. Will you help me _____ pack the boxes?

16. Mom was _____ pleased with my grades.

17. Mr. Baker _____ locked the door.

18. Ollie _____ agrees with me.

Word Building

> *Im-, in-,* and *re-* are prefixes. The prefixes *im-* and *in-* mean "not." *Im-* is used before a base word beginning with *m* or *p,* as in *improper.* The prefix *re-* means "again," as in *rerun.*

Practice Read each word. Circle the base word. Draw a line under the prefix.

1. redo

2. incomplete

3. inactive

4. impure

5. replay

6. insane

7. refill

8. imperfect

9. improper

10. refresh

11. reheat

12. remake

Apply Add a prefix to each of the following words to make a new word.

re-   in-   im-

13. _____ polite

14. _____ exact

15. _____ call

16. _____ tell

17. _____ dependent

18. _____ mortal

19. _____ heat

20. _____ place

21. _____ visible

22. _____ valid

23. _____ possible

24. _____ set

Sounds and Spellings Review

Practice Draw a line to match the picture to the correct word. Write the word beside the picture.

1. pant

2. wax

3. paint

4. grass

5. wakes

6. bait

Apply Write the correct word to complete each sentence.

race	day	tank	wait	flat	flag

7. Dan fills the _____ with gas.

8. He makes sure the tires are not _____.

9. His car is ready for the _____.

10. Cars line up and _____ for a signal.

11. A _____ is waved, and cars take off!

12. It is a good _____ for a car race.

Phonics • *Skills Practice*

Sounds and Spellings Review

Practice Write the words that have the same vowel sound as each picture.

spine	might	mitt	pilot
dries	twin	pickle	knit

_____

_____

_____

_____

_____

Apply Write the word that correctly completes each sentence.

sniff	tries	kitten
climb	high	hides

1. We have a _____ named Cricket.

2. She likes to _____ flowers.

3. She will _____ up tree trunks.

4. Cricket likes to be up _____.

5. She _____ to catch tiny bugs.

6. Cricket _____ under the ivy to take a nap.

Phonics • *Skills Practice*

Sounds and Spellings Review
Practice Write the word that names each picture.
Then write two more words that rhyme with that word.

| rope | toast | mop | sock |

1.

2.

3.

4.

Apply Read each riddle and write the answer. You will not use all the words.

doll   phone   frog

poem   fox   bolt

5. I am an animal.
I live in the forest.
I belong to the dog family.
What am I?

_____

6. I am made up of words.
You can write me.
You can read me.
What am I?

_____

7. I have many meanings.
I can be a flash of lightning.
I can hold things together.
What am I?

_____

8. I have buttons you press.
You use me to speak to pals.
I can send a text message.
What am I?

_____

     Phonics • *Skills Practice*

Sounds and Spellings Review

Practice Write the word from the word box that means almost the same thing as each numbered word.

bug	smudge	human	tumble
music	shrub	cube	crunch

1. fall _____

2. plant _____

3. smear _____

4. chew _____

5. block _____

6. person _____

7. insect _____

8. tune _____

Apply **Read the sentences and circle the words with the short *u* or long *u* sound. Write each word under the correct column.**

Matt and a few boys were at lunch. Matt was hungry. He looked at a menu and ordered a sandwich. When the sub came, it was huge!

Short *u*

_____

_____

_____

_____

Long *u*

_____

_____

_____

Sounds and Spellings Review

| sleepy tread reason meter speckled heading |

Practice Read each word. Write the word in the correct column to tell if the e has the long or short sound.

Short e

Long e

_____

_____

_____

_____

_____

_____

_____

_____

Apply Read the story. Write the correct word to complete each sentence.

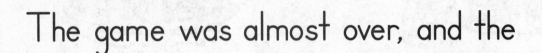

cheered   season   even   field   pep   fence

It was the last game of the

_____

_____. Coach Reed gave

us a _____ talk.

The game was almost over, and the

score was _____. Then Gene hit the

ball over the _____. It landed in a

grassy _____. It was a

homerun! The team

_____

_____ loudly.

Phonics • *Skills Practice*

Sounds and Spellings Review

Digraphs are two or more letters that
make one sound.

Practice **Read each sentence. Circle the word with the consonant digraph. Write the digraph on the line.**

1. We ate brunch at home. _____

2. Dad put milk into a pitcher. _____

3. Melinda drew strange shapes. _____

4. Bart pointed to the chart. _____

5. We ate fresh strawberries. _____

6. Mom took some family photos. _____

Apply Read or listen to each riddle. Write the correct word on the line.

chair   alphabet   sunshine   clothing

7. I make words.
   I have vowels and consonants.
   I have 26 letters.
   What am I?

   _____

8. You sit on me.
   I can be wood or plastic.
   I have four legs.
   What am I?

   _____

9. You wear me.
   I can be pants.
   I can be a shirt.
   What am I?

   _____

10. You see me on clear days.
    I am bright.
    I help plants grow.
    What am I?

    _____

Phonics • *Skills Practice*

Sounds and Spellings Review

chirp	farmer	star	storyteller
curry	circle	gurgle	popcorn

Practice Read each category. Write the words that belong under each category.

Food

_____

_ _ _ _ _ _ _ _ _ _ _ _ _ _ _ _ _ _

_____

_ _ _ _ _ _ _ _ _ _ _ _ _ _ _ _ _ _

_____

People

_____

_ _ _ _ _ _ _ _ _ _ _ _ _ _ _ _ _ _

_____

_ _ _ _ _ _ _ _ _ _ _ _ _ _ _ _ _ _

_____

Sounds

_____

_ _ _ _ _ _ _ _ _ _ _ _ _ _ _ _ _ _

_____

_ _ _ _ _ _ _ _ _ _ _ _ _ _ _ _ _ _

_____

Shapes

_____

_ _ _ _ _ _ _ _ _ _ _ _ _ _ _ _ _ _

_____

_ _ _ _ _ _ _ _ _ _ _ _ _ _ _ _ _ _

_____

Apply Write the correct word to complete the sentences in the story.

swirled	shore	surrounded	storm

There would not be a _____ at the

coast today. We played along the sandy

_____. Gentle waves _____

around our feet. We smiled as seagulls

_____ the bread crumbs that

we tossed on the sand.

Phonics • *Skills Practice*

Sounds and Spellings Review
Practice Unscramble the letters and write the word on the line.

1. c w e r

2. n u r p e

3. a u t b

4. o t o d s

5. o b o k

6. o s p c o

7. f o h o

8. d g o o

Apply **Look at each picture. Read the sentence.
Write the word that rhymes with the underlined word
to correctly complete each sentence.**

| hood | broom | cook | moon |

9. We will <u>soon</u> see the _____ .

10. Take a <u>look</u> at the _____ .

11. Bill swept the <u>room</u>

with a _____ .

12. A <u>good</u> raincoat has a _____

Sounds and Spellings Review

point	crowds	enjoy	playground
noise	avoid	pounce	houses

Practice **Read the headings. Write each word under the correct category.**

Action Words

_____

- - - - - - - - - - - - - - -

_____

- - - - - - - - - - - - - - -

_____

- - - - - - - - - - - - - - -

_____

Things in a City

_____

- - - - - - - - - - - - - - -

_____

- - - - - - - - - - - - - - -

_____

- - - - - - - - - - - - - - -

_____

Apply Write the correct word to complete each sentence in the story.

crown town loud
crowd loyal tower

The queen heard _____ cheers.

She put on her velvet cape and jeweled _____ .

She went to look out a window in the _____ .

Below she saw a large _____ .

The people of the _____ would always be _____ to her.

Phonics • *Skills Practice*

Word Building

Practice Add an inflectional ending to each action word. Write the new word in the space provided.

1. talk + s = _____

2. jump + ed = _____

3. look + ing = _____

4. learn + ed = _____

5. play + s = _____

6. start + ing = _____

Apply Read each sentence. Write the correct word endings to complete the words.

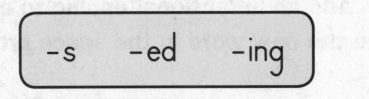

| -s | -ed | -ing |

7. My dad run _____ before work.

8. Hannah is cook _____ dinner.

9. Mr. Jones lock _____ the door when he left.

10. Ken walk _____ past my house last night.

11. The puppy is chew _____ on a slipper.

12. Jane take _____ a sandwich for lunch.